Date: 7/27/12

J 513.26 ATW
Atwood, Megan.
Cuddly kittens : discovering
fractions /

CUDDLY KITTENS: DISCOVERING FRACTIONS

by Megan Atwood

illustrated by Sharon Holm

Content Consultant: Paula J. Maida, PhD

magic wagon

Published by Magic Wagon, a division of the ABDO Group, PO Box 398166, Minneapolis, MN 55439. Copyright © 2012 by Abdo Consulting Group, Inc. International copyrights reserved in all countries. All rights reserved. No part of this book may be reproduced in any form without written permission from the publisher.

Looking Glass Library™ is a trademark and logo of Magic Wagon.

Printed in the United States of America, North Mankato, Minnesota.
102011
012012

 THIS BOOK CONTAINS AT LEAST 10% RECYCLED MATERIALS.

Text by Megan Atwood
Illustrations by Sharon Holm
Edited by Lisa Owings
Interior layout and design by Christa Schneider
Cover design by Christa Schneider

Library of Congress Cataloging-in-Publication Data

Atwood, Megan.
  Cuddly kittens : discovering fractions / by Megan Atwood ; illustrated by Sharon Lane Holm.
      p. cm. — (Count the critters)
  ISBN 978-1-61641-853-3
  1. Fractions — Juvenile literature. I. Holm, Sharon Lane, ill. II. Title.
  QA117.A89 2012
  513.2'6 — dc23
                        2011033075

Fractions are fun! Four cuddly
kittens are going to homes to be
loved. Let's learn about fractions
as these kittens get adopted.
We will learn:
one-fourth: 1/4
one-third: 1/3
one-half: 1/2

Kittens pounce and play. These four kittens make one whole litter. They pounce on their toys and each other.

one whole 4/4=1

They creep across the floor
and spring into the air. Count
them: one, two, three, four.

one-fourth 1/4

Kittens play and pounce. Four kittens play together. They run and jump and roll. It's fun to be a kitten! One of the four kittens is going to a home to be loved. One-fourth of the litter is adopted!

Kittens prance and purr. Three
kittens prance around their toys.
They walk proudly on their toes.
Count the kittens: one, two, three.

one whole 3/3=1

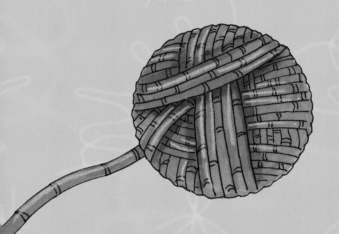

Kittens purr and prance. Three kittens purr to show they are pleased. They purr breathing out and they purr breathing in. One of the three kittens is going to a home to be loved. One-third of the kittens are adopted!

Kittens clean and cuddle each other. Two sleepy kittens curl up and cuddle. It's time for a bath!

one whole $2/2=1$

Kitten tongues have tiny spines that help them clean and comb each other. Count the kittens: one, two.

Kittens cuddle and clean each other.
Two cuddly kittens kiss each other
good-bye. One of the two kittens is
going to a home to be loved.
One-half of the kittens are adopted!

one-half   **1/2**

One whole **1/1=1**

Kittens mewl and meow. The last lonely kitten mewls for his friends. Where have all the other kittens gone?

Kittens meow and mewl. Four happy kittens meow when they see each other. They greet each other with their tails held high. The whole litter is going to the same home!

One whole 4/4=1

Kittens pounce and play, prance and purr, cuddle and clean each other, and mewl and meow. One whole happy family of cats is adopted!

one whole 4/4=1

Now you know fractions.

And all the kittens are loved!

1/2 4/4=1

Words to Know

adopted—taken in as one's own.

litter—a group of animals born at the same time.

mewl—to cry softly.

pounce—to jump on something.

prance—to walk in a happy way.

purr—the sound a cat makes when it is happy.

Web Sites

To learn more about fractions, visit ABDO Group online at **www.abdopublishing.com**. Web sites about fractions are featured on our Book Links page. These links are routinely monitored and updated to provide the most current information available.

1/4 1/3 1/2